Centerville Library
Washington-Centerville Public Library
Centerville, Ohio

DISCARD

W9-AHO-360

· DELICIOUS ·

DUMP CAKES

· DELICIOUS ·
DUMP CAKES

50 Super Simple Desserts to Make in 15 Minutes or Less

ROXANNE WYSS AND **KATHY MOORE**

PHOTOGRAPHS BY STACI VALENTINE

ST. MARTIN'S GRIFFIN
NEW YORK

*Dedicated to busy families everywhere,
who gather to share love and good food
around the table*

DELICIOUS DUMP CAKES. Copyright © 2016 by Roxanne Wyss and
Kathy Moore. Photographs © 2016 by Staci Valentine. All rights reserved.
Printed in China. For information, address St. Martin's Press, 175 Fifth
Avenue, New York, N.Y. 10010.

www.stmartins.com

Book design: Rita Sowins / Sowins Design
Food stylist: Jeanne Kelley

The Library of Congress Cataloging-in-Publication Data is available upon
request.

ISBN 978-1-250-08263-3 (trade paperback)

ISBN 978-1-250-08264-0 (e-book)

Our books may be purchased in bulk for promotional, educational,
or business use. Please contact your local bookseller or the Macmillan
Corporate and Premium Sales Department at 1-800-221-7945, extension
5442, or by e-mail at MacmillanSpecialMarkets@macmillan.com.

First Edition: May 2016

10 9 8 7 6 5

✴ *Contents* ✴

Flavorful Fruits … 51

Caramel and Ooey-Gooey Treats … 77

Specialty Dump Cakes ... 93

Acknowledgments ... 114

✳ *Dump Cake Basics* ✳

DELICIOUS DUMP CAKES is a mouthwatering collection of no-fuss desserts that taste fantastic and that you prepare in just minutes. Now anyone can bake the best rich, wonderful, and comforting desserts and get out of the kitchen with lightning-quick speed.

Let's face it, not everyone is a gourmet cook, but everyone eats, and very few can resist dessert. This book takes fantastic desserts away from pastry chefs and puts them into the hands of today's busy home cooks. Simplicity and efficiency combined with great flavor make each of these layered treats a winner!

Delicious Dump Cakes features a wide array of super-easy, great-tasting cakes and desserts. For nearly all of the recipes, just layer the ingredients in the pan. For a few, you may need to prepare a pudding mix or something equally simple, but you will never have to struggle with complex steps or lots of dirty dishes.

Most people credit a simple combination of a can of cherry pie filling and a can of crushed pineapple, layered in a 9 x 13-inch pan and topped with a yellow cake mix and butter as the first dump cake. Scouts may remember baking this treat in a Dutch oven over a campfire, and many will remember when tables at church potlucks and family reunions were lined with pans of this popular dessert.

It is a tasty cake, but why stop there? The flavor combinations are nearly endless, and this collection presents a wide array of dump cakes. The only hard part is trying to select your favorite.

It's as Easy as 1-2-3

1. Layer the ingredients evenly in the pan in the order listed. Do not stir unless specifically directed to do so in the recipe.
2. Bake in a preheated oven for the time listed. Typically, the oven is preheated to 350°F.
3. Allow to cool for 15 to 30 minutes, then enjoy.

Tips for the Best Results

+ Use the size of the pan listed in the recipe. For most of the recipes, that is a 9 x 13-inch baking pan. Either a metal pan or glass baking dish can be used.
+ Spray the pan with nonstick cooking spray.
+ Spread the ingredients evenly.
+ Canned pie filling and crushed pineapple may have been the first fruits used in dump cakes, but other fruits can now be used. Dump cakes today may include layers of other canned fruits as well as pieces of fresh or frozen fruit. The recipes specify whether to use the liquid when using canned fruit.
+ Cake mix is often used dry or just sprinkled out of the box evenly into the pan. Break up any lumps in the dry cake mix. A fork makes this easy to do.
+ Many dump cakes include nuts, chocolate chips, crushed candy bars, or other flavor additions. Be sure to sprinkle these evenly over the cake mix.
+ Moisten all the cake mix with the liquid or the butter. Drizzle the liquid or melted butter slowly so it seeps into the cake mix.
+ Some recipes will suggest you stir or blend ingredients together. These dump cakes are often chocolate or other flavors that are not layered with fruit. For these recipes, the dry cake mix is frequently blended with an instant pudding mix and milk or another liquid.

Delicious Dump Cakes

- Some recipes suggest blending the ingredients in a mixing bowl and others blending them right in the baking pan. It is your choice whether to blend in the pan or a bowl. A mixing bowl is very convenient, but blending in the pan means one less bowl to wash. If you blend in the pan, be sure to get into the corners of the pan and blend all the ingredients. A rubber spatula will help you get into the corners of the pan.
- When done, the top of the dump cake will be golden brown and lightly set. The cake may begin to pull away from the sides of the pan.
- Allow dump cakes to cool for 15 to 30 minutes before serving.
- Dump cakes are often best served while slightly warm, and are ideally served on the same day they are made.
- Store leftover dump cakes made with fruit, pudding, or cream in the refrigerator. If you wish to reheat a dump cake, only reheat those without frosting or whipped topping. Reheat the dump cake, uncovered, in a 350°F oven for 10 to 15 minutes, or until warm.
- Dump cakes are especially good topped with a scoop of ice cream, whipped cream, or thawed frozen whipped topping. You can top dump cakes with your favorite frosting, but many dump cakes are sweet and moist enough that they do not need frosting.

Basic Ingredients for Dump Cakes

BUTTER

Choose unsalted (sweet) butter.

Some recipes will recommend melted butter. Drizzle the melted butter very slowly over the cake so it seeps in and moistens the entire cake mix.

Other recipes will suggest slicing the cold butter into very thin slivers. Butter is easier to slice into slivers if you use a thin, sharp knife and the butter is well chilled. Arrange the slivers over the top of the cake mix, distributing them as evenly as possible and covering the top of the cake completely.

Low-fat, light, soft, whipped, or tubs of butter all have a different formulation than sticks of butter and are not recommended for these recipes, as the texture and the flavor of the dump cake may be adversely affected.

CAKE MIX

Many dump cake recipes begin with a cake mix while some even begin with a muffin mix, bar cookie mix, or other mix.

Sprinkle the dry cake mix into the prepared pan. Spread the cake mix evenly, breaking up any lumps.

Cake mixes are available in both two-layer- and one-layer-size packages. Cake mixes sized to make two-layer cakes are commonly used for dump cakes, but occasionally the smaller, one-layer cake mix is recommended. Follow the recipe recommendation for the best results.

The package weight for many two-layer cake mixes ranges from 15.25 to 18 ounces, especially for such common flavors such as yellow, chocolate, and vanilla cake. The national brands, including Betty Crocker, Pillsbury, and Duncan Hines, and many store brands generally seem to fall within this range and this is the weight range used for testing these recipes. Some flavors, specifically lemon, caramel, and red velvet cake mixes, range in weight from 16 to 19 ounces. When selecting a cake mix, we recommend using one of approximately the same weight as that listed in the recipe. The exact weight of the mix varies with the brand and the flavor and we have found that the slight deviations do not affect the baking and still produce great cakes.

Those cake mixes with pudding in the mix (often labeled "extra moist") and those without pudding work equally well. Use either type of cake mix for the dump cake recipes in this book. If the dump cake recipe you are using recommends blending the cake mix into a pudding mix, and your cake mix

lists that it has pudding in it, go ahead and blend it into a separate package of pudding mix just as the recipe recommends.

You will spot several brands of cake mix on the grocery store shelf; experiment a little to determine which you enjoy the most.

Can you interchange flavors? Sure, but we recommend you choose a similar flavor for the best results. For example, if the recipe lists devil's food cake and you choose to use a chocolate cake mix, the dump cake recipe will work fine. Similarly a yellow and a white cake mix can be interchanged.

Stock up on the cake mixes when they are on sale. Be sure to double-check the date code and use the cake mixes before they expire.

See pages 10 to 13 on how to make your own mix.

MILK AND OTHER LIQUIDS

Some recipes recommend a can of evaporated milk, while others list half-and-half. These can be used interchangeably as long as you use the same amount. You can also substitute an equal amount of fresh, whole milk for the evaporated milk or half-and-half.

Other liquids, such as fruit juice, liquor, or wine, are listed in the recipes and work great in dump cakes. You can substitute liquids, such as using fruit juice for bourbon or wine, and they will work nicely but such changes may alter the flavor or the texture of the dump cake slightly.

PECANS, WALNUTS, AND OTHER NUTS

Toasting the pecans, walnuts, or other nuts intensifies their flavor. To toast the nuts, spread them out in a single layer on a rimmed baking sheet. Bake at 350°F for 5 to 7 minutes or until lightly toasted.

✳ *Make Your Own Cake Mix* ✳

Making your own cake mix is quick, easy, and economical. The concept of blending a mix is an old one—and flyers from university extension services from the 1940s and 1950s included a recipe called "The Master Mix," which was a basic blend that you could use for making cakes and other baked goods.

While classic, making your own mix is as current and timely as the next Pinterest pin. Just blend a few basic ingredients and you will have a great mix to use when baking a dump cake. Not only is it convenient to make your own mix, you can control the quality and avoid certain allergens or chemicals if you prefer. Best of all, they taste great.

The mixes can be stored at room temperature in a tightly sealed container for up to 3 months. It is especially convenient to mix up several batches of cake mix at once so you will have them ready to go whenever you want to make a dump cake.

Make Your Own Yellow Cake Mix

Use this handy mix any time a recipe calls for yellow cake mix.

2¼ cups all-purpose flour
1¾ cups sugar
⅓ cup nonfat dry milk powder
1 tablespoon baking powder
1 teaspoon salt

In a large bowl, whisk all the ingredients together. Store in an airtight container.

Use this in place of one purchased, two-layer-size boxed cake mix in your favorite dump cake recipe that calls for a yellow cake mix.

tips: Measure the ingredients accurately. Spoon the flour or sugar into a dry measuring cup and level off the top with a table knife.

If preparing a recipe that calls for a one-layer cake mix, measure out and use 2 cups plus 3 tablespoons of this mix.

Make Your Own Old-Fashioned White Cake Mix

This old-fashioned white cake mix makes a great dump cake and you can use it any time the recipe calls for a white cake mix. The shortening adds wonderful moisture and richness to the dump cake.

3 cups all-purpose flour
1½ cups sugar
⅓ cup nonfat dry milk powder
4 teaspoons baking powder
1 teaspoon salt
¾ cup shortening

In a large bowl, whisk together the flour, sugar, dry milk powder, baking powder, and salt. Cut in the shortening, using a pastry cutter or two knives, until the mixture forms coarse, even crumbs. Store in an airtight container.

Use this in place of one purchased, two-layer-size boxed cake mix in your favorite dump cake recipe that calls for a white cake mix.

tips: If desired, combine the flour, sugar, dry milk powder, baking powder, and salt in the work bowl of a food processor and pulse to blend. Add the shortening and pulse until the mixture forms coarse, even crumbs.

If preparing a recipe that calls for a one-layer cake mix, measure out and use 2¾ cups of this mix.

Make Your Own Chocolate Cake Mix

Don't ever be in a pinch again. Just blend a few simple pantry ingredients together and you will have a great chocolate cake mix for a dump cake.

1¾ cups all-purpose flour

1½ cups sugar

¾ cup unsweetened cocoa powder

⅓ cup nonfat dry milk powder

1½ teaspoons baking powder

1 teaspoon baking soda

1 teaspoon salt

In a large bowl, whisk all of the ingredients together. Store in an airtight container.

Use this in place of one purchased, two-layer-size boxed cake mix in your favorite dump cake recipe that calls for a chocolate cake mix.

tips: For the unsweetened cocoa powder in this recipe, choose natural cocoa powder, those typically found in the grocery store by such brands as Hershey's and Nestle. This kind of cocoa is made from cocoa beans that were roasted and pulverized to make the fine powder. Dutch-process cocoa is not recommended for this recipe.

If preparing a recipe that calls for a one-layer cake mix, measure out and use 2 cups plus 3 tablespoons of this mix.

Classic Dump Cakes

Rocky Road Dump Cake

MAKES 1 (9 X 13-INCH) CAKE

A Rocky Road Dump Cake trumps rocky road ice cream any day of the week. Of course, you can always serve this with a scoop of vanilla ice cream on top.

Nonstick cooking spray
1 (15.25- to 18-ounce) box chocolate cake mix
1 (3.9-ounce) package chocolate instant pudding mix
1¾ cups whole milk
1 cup semisweet chocolate chips
1½ cups mini marshmallows
1 cup chopped pecans

Preheat the oven to 350°F. Spray a 9 x 13-inch pan with nonstick cooking spray.

In a large bowl, stir together the cake mix, pudding mix, and milk until smooth. Spoon the batter into the prepared pan and spread evenly. Sprinkle evenly with the chocolate chips, then sprinkle evenly with the marshmallows. Sprinkle the top evenly with the pecans.

Bake for 25 to 30 minutes or until the edges of the cake begin to pull away from the sides of the pan.

Serve warm or at room temperature.

tip: Substitute regular-size marshmallows for the mini version by simply cutting the large marshmallows into fourths; measure 1½ cups of the cut marshmallows and proceed as the recipe directs.

Brownie Turtle Pecan Dump Cake

MAKES 1 (9 X 13-INCH) CAKE

This Brownie Turtle Pecan Dump Cake is guaranteed to stop any cravings you might have to visit your local candy shop. You can replicate candy in an easy-to-make and easy-to-serve dessert and please all the sweet tooths in your home!

Nonstick cooking spray
¾ cup (1½ sticks) unsalted butter, melted
2 cups milk chocolate chips
1 (15.25- to 18-ounce) box German chocolate cake mix
½ cup thick butterscotch-caramel topping (see tips)
1 cup coarsely chopped pecans, toasted
1 (12-ounce) can evaporated milk

Preheat the oven to 350°F. Spray a 9 x 13-inch baking pan with nonstick cooking spray.

Pour ¼ cup of the melted butter into the prepared pan and tilt the pan to coat the bottom evenly. Sprinkle 1 cup of the milk chocolate chips evenly over the melted butter.

Sprinkle half of the cake mix evenly over the milk chocolate chips. Drizzle the caramel topping evenly over the cake mix. Sprinkle the pecans and the remaining 1 cup milk chocolate chips evenly over all. Sprinkle the remaining cake mix evenly over all.

Pour the evaporated milk evenly over all. Drizzle the remaining ½ cup butter evenly over the top.

Bake for 40 to 45 minutes or until the edges of the cake begin to pull away from the sides of the pan.

tips: Ice cream topping or syrup? While similar, those labeled "ice cream topping" are thicker than syrups. For the best results for this recipe, choose a thick ice cream topping. We prefer Mrs. Richardson's brand Butterscotch Caramel topping as it gave the best results.

Substitute Nestle's 9-ounce package Delightfulls (caramel-filled baking morsels) for the milk chocolate chips. Omit the caramel sauce and proceed as directed.

Serve this cake with a scoop of vanilla ice cream or a dollop of whipped cream for an over-the-top dessert.

Do you prefer milk chocolate or would you choose dark chocolate or semisweet chocolate? You can substitute semi-sweet or dark chocolate chips for the milk choco-late chips in this recipe.

German Chocolate Dump Cake

MAKES 1 (9 X 13-INCH) CAKE

A classic German Chocolate Cake features the luscious flavors of chocolate, pecans, and coconut and this quick-and-easy version doesn't disappoint at all.

Nonstick cooking spray
1 (14-ounce) can sweetened condensed milk
1 (12-ounce) package semisweet chocolate chips
1 cup sweetened flaked coconut
1 cup pecan pieces, toasted
1 (15.25- to 18-ounce) box German chocolate cake mix
1 cup (2 sticks) unsalted butter, melted
Whipped cream for serving, optional

Preheat the oven to 350°F. Spray a 9 x 13-inch pan with nonstick cooking spray.

Pour the sweetened condensed milk into the prepared pan and spread it evenly. Sprinkle evenly with the chocolate chips, coconut, and pecans. Sprinkle the cake mix evenly over the pecans. Drizzle the melted butter evenly over the cake mix.

Bake for 35 to 40 minutes or until the cake is set and golden brown. Allow to cool for at least 10 minutes.

Serve warm, topped with a dollop of whipped cream, if desired.

Chocolate Chip Cookie Dough Dump Cake

MAKES 1 (9 X 13-INCH) CAKE

What is your favorite sweet treat? Is it a cake, or do you prefer cookies? You won't have to decide which you prefer when you make this Chocolate Chip Cookie Dough Dump Cake for dessert, for it will remind you of both. Luscious mounds of cookie dough swirled in a chocolate cake—what could be better?

Nonstick cooking spray
1 (3.9-ounce) package chocolate instant pudding mix
1¾ cups whole milk
1 (15.25- to 18-ounce) box devil's food cake mix
1 (16½-ounce) package refrigerated and prepared chocolate chip cookie dough

tip: Substitute peanut butter or chocolate–peanut butter cookie dough for the chocolate chip cookie dough.

Preheat the oven to 350°F. Spray a 9 x 13-inch pan with nonstick cooking spray.

Pour the pudding mix into the prepared pan. Add the milk and whisk until the pudding is thick and creamy, about 2 minutes. Stir in the cake mix and blend until moistened. Spread the batter evenly in the pan.

Cut the cookie dough into ½- to ¾-inch cubes. Scatter the cookie dough evenly over the cake batter.

Bake for 40 to 45 minutes or until a wooden pick inserted in the center of the cake comes out clean.

Chocolate Chip Cookie Dough Dump Cake Cupcakes

MAKES 24 CUPCAKES

Preheat the oven to 350°F. Spray 24 muffin cups with nonstick cooking spray.

Prepare the Chocolate Chip Cookie Dough batter, in a mixing bowl, as directed in the recipe (on page 22).

Fill each muffin cup half full.

Cut the cookie dough into ⅜-inch cubes. Distribute the cubes of cookie dough evenly over the cupcakes.

Bake for 25 to 30 minutes or until a wooden pick inserted in the center of the cupcakes comes out clean.

Red Velvet Dump Cake with Original Old-Fashioned Frosting

MAKES 1 (9 X 13-INCH) CAKE

Food historians cannot agree on the origin of the bright red, tender-crumbed cake. We can all agree that it is one of the most requested cakes for celebrations. The cooked frosting is a favorite in the South, and once you give this frosting a try you will see why southerners adore the cooked sweet creation on top of their bright red cake.

Nonstick cooking spray
1 (16- to 19-ounce) box red velvet cake mix
1 (3.4-ounce) package cheesecake or vanilla instant pudding mix
1½ cups whole milk

ORIGINAL OLD-FASHIONED FROSTING
⅔ cup whole milk
2 tablespoons all-purpose flour
¼ teaspoon salt
⅔ cup sugar
⅔ cup (10⅔ tablespoons) unsalted butter, at room temperature
1 teaspoon pure vanilla extract

Preheat the oven to 350°F. Spray a 9 x 13-inch pan with nonstick cooking spray.

Sprinkle the cake mix evenly in the prepared pan. Sprinkle evenly with the pudding mix. Pour the milk into the dry mixes. Using a fork, blend the mixes and milk together until smooth.

Bake for 30 to 35 minutes or until a wooden pick inserted in the center of the cake comes out clean. Allow to cool completely before frosting.

(continued)

tips: By all means, you can omit the cooked frosting and substitute your favorite cream cheese frosting.

Add 1 cup premium white chips to the batter and bake the cake as directed.

MAKE THE FROSTING: Combine the milk, flour, and salt in a small saucepan over medium heat. Cook, stirring continuously, until the mixture thickens and comes to a boil, about 5 minutes.

Boil for 1 minute and remove from the heat. Pour into a small bowl and cover with plastic wrap. Allow to cool completely, at least 1 hour.

In a large bowl, combine the sugar, butter, and vanilla. Using an electric mixer, beat at medium speed until creamy. Add the cooled flour mixture and continue to beat until the frosting is light and fluffy.

Frost the red velvet cake with the Original Old-Fashioned Frosting.

Triple Berry Cobbler

MAKES 1 (9 X 13-INCH) CAKE

The Triple Berry Cobbler is a foolproof recipe for large gatherings of friends and family. Sunday dinner for guests? The family reunion? The book club at your home? You have it covered!

Nonstick cooking spray
2 (16-ounce) bags frozen mixed berries
1 (15.25- to 18-ounce) box French vanilla cake mix
12 to 16-ounces lemon-lime carbonated soda
Vanilla ice cream for serving, optional

tip: You can substitute white or yellow cake mix for the French vanilla.

Preheat the oven to 350°F. Spray a 9 x 13-inch pan with nonstick cooking spray.

Place the frozen mixed berries in a single layer in the prepared pan. Sprinkle the cake mix evenly over the berries. Pour 1½ cups of the lemon-lime soda evenly over the cake mix. Allow to stand for 5 minutes.

Using the remaining soda as needed, pour the soda over any dry areas to saturate all of the cake mix.

Bake the cake for 45 to 50 minutes or until bubbling and golden. This is best served warm with a scoop of vanilla ice cream.

Hawaiian Dump Cake

MAKES 1 (9 X 13-INCH) CAKE

We live in the Midwest where winters can be harsh and cabin fever can be contracted very easily. When the doldrums arrive, prepare this tropical treat and you will swear you see palm trees swaying.

Nonstick cooking spray
1 (20-ounce) can crushed pineapple in juice
1 (15-ounce) can cream of coconut
½ cup maraschino cherries, well drained and cut in half
1 (15.25- to 18-ounce) box yellow cake mix
1 cup (2 sticks) unsalted butter, sliced into slivers

Preheat the oven to 350°F. Spray a 9 x 13-inch pan with nonstick cooking spray.

Pour the pineapple with the juice evenly into the prepared pan. Spoon the cream of coconut evenly over the pineapple. Sprinkle the maraschino cherries evenly over all. Sprinkle the cake mix evenly over the fruit. Distribute the butter slivers evenly over the top.

Bake the cake for 40 to 45 minutes or until golden. Cool completely before serving.

tips: If you like a little more crunch, sprinkle the cream of coconut with about ⅔ cup of sweetened, flaked coconut and proceed as the recipe directs.

Canned cream of coconut is a thick, sweet mixture commonly sold for cocktails. It is typically found in the mixed drink section of your grocery store. It should not be confused with coconut milk.

Banana Split Dump Cake

MAKES 1 (9 X 13-INCH) CAKE

Am I the only one who can't eat the traditional banana split without spilling syrup and ice cream all over as I attempt to cut the banana boat slices? No more trouble for me! This Banana Split Dump Cake saves the day when we crave an old-fashioned banana split. It is so much better and it is an easy way to enjoy all the flavors with a scoop of ice cream on top! No spills to clean up . . . ahh, life is good!

Nonstick cooking spray
2 bananas
2 cups sliced fresh strawberries
1 (20-ounce) can crushed pineapple in juice
½ cup mini semisweet chocolate chips
1 (15.25- to 18-ounce) box white cake mix
⅔ cup chopped pecans
½ cup (1 stick) unsalted butter, melted
Whipped cream or vanilla ice cream for serving
12 maraschino cherries, drained

tip: Omit the mini chocolate chips in the recipe. After dolloping with whipped cream or ice cream, drizzle chocolate ice cream syrup over all and top each serving with a maraschino cherry.

Preheat the oven to 350°F. Spray a 9 x 13-inch pan with nonstick cooking spray.

Slice the bananas crosswise, about ¼ inch thick, and layer them evenly on the bottom of the prepared pan. Layer the sliced strawberries evenly over the bananas. Pour the pineapple with the juice evenly over the strawberries. Sprinkle the mini chocolate chips evenly over the fruit. Sprinkle the cake mix evenly over the chocolate chips. Sprinkle the pecans evenly over all. Drizzle the melted butter evenly over the top.

Bake the cake for 40 to 45 minutes or until set and golden.

When ready to serve, spoon the cake into individual bowls, dollop with whipped cream or ice cream, and top with a cherry.

✳ Chocolate ✳

Mississippi Mud Dump Cake

MAKES 1 (9 X 13-INCH) CAKE

Roxanne spent her childhood summers at the family cabin at the Lake of the Ozarks in Missouri. Almost every weekend included boating, skiing, fishing, and enjoying a version of this cake as a weekend treat. You don't need to be at the lake to make a Mississippi Mud Dump Cake; enjoy it any day of the week.

Nonstick cooking spray
1½ cups whole milk
1 (5.9-ounce) package chocolate instant pudding mix
1 (15.25- to 18-ounce) box devil's food cake mix
1 (7½-ounce) jar marshmallow crème

MISSISSIPPI MUD FROSTING
½ cup (1 stick) unsalted butter
3 tablespoons unsweetened cocoa powder
6 tablespoons whole milk
4 cups confectioners' sugar
1 cup coarsely chopped pecans, toasted
1 teaspoon pure vanilla extract

Preheat the oven to 350°F. Spray a 9 x 13-inch pan with nonstick cooking spray.

In a large bowl, whisk together the milk and the pudding mix until smooth. Stir in the cake mix. Pour the batter into the prepared pan and spread evenly.

Bake for 30 to 35 minutes or until a wooden pick inserted in the center of the cake comes out clean.

(continued)

When the cake comes out of the oven, dollop the marshmallow crème on the warm cake. Using a knife or spreader, carefully spread it over the entire cake.

MAKE THE FROSTING: Heat the butter, cocoa, and milk in a medium saucepan and cook over medium-high heat, stirring occasionally, until the butter has melted. Bring to a boil, remove from the heat, add the confectioners' sugar, and whisk until smooth. Stir in the pecans and vanilla. Pour over the warm cake and spread to coat evenly.

Chocolate Pudding Dump Cake

MAKES 1 (9 X 13-INCH) CAKE

Do you embrace all things chocolate and never think about other flavors of dessert? You are not alone, for lots of people are true "chocoholics." We will vouch that this Chocolate Pudding Dump Cake is the perfect dessert for all of the pure chocolate lovers. The coffee intensifies the flavor of the chocolate, but trust us, you won't taste the coffee. If you really are a purist, omit the coffee and increase the milk to 1¾ cups.

Nonstick cooking spray
1 (3.9-ounce) package chocolate instant pudding mix
1½ cups whole milk
¼ cup hot brewed coffee
1 (15.25- to 18-ounce) box devil's food cake mix
1 cup semisweet chocolate chips
¼ cup (½ stick) unsalted butter, sliced into slivers

Preheat the oven to 350°F. Spray a 9 x 13-inch pan with nonstick cooking spray.

Pour the pudding mix into the prepared pan. Add the milk and coffee and whisk until the pudding is thick and creamy, about 2 minutes. Stir in the cake mix and blend until moistened. Spread the batter evenly in the pan. Sprinkle the chocolate chips evenly over the cake batter. Distribute the butter slivers evenly over the top.

Bake for 35 to 40 minutes or until the edges of the cake begin to pull away from the sides of the pan.

Malted Milk Ball Dump Cake

MAKES 1 (9 X 13-INCH) CAKE

Roxanne's daughter delights in eating malted milk balls. Imagine how thrilled she was when this recipe was developed, crossing a malted milk shake with her grandma's old-fashioned chocolate cake. Smiles emerged all around the dinner table!

Nonstick cooking spray
1 (15.25- to 18-ounce) box dark chocolate or devil's food cake mix
1 (3.9-ounce) package chocolate instant pudding mix
1¾ cups whole milk
2 cups malted milk balls
1 cup semisweet chocolate chips
Whipped cream or ice cream for serving, optional

Preheat the oven to 350°F. Spray a 9 x 13-inch pan with nonstick cooking spray.

In a large bowl, combine the cake mix, pudding mix, and milk and mix until blended thoroughly; the mixture will be thick. Stir in the malted milk balls and the chocolate chips. Spoon into the prepared pan and level the top of the batter evenly.

Bake for 30 to 35 minutes or until the edges of the cake begin to pull away from the sides of the pan.

This is great served warm or at room temperature. Serve with whipped cream or ice cream dolloped on top if you like.

Everyone's Favorite Cookie Dump Cake

MAKES 1 (9 X 13-INCH) CAKE

Those classic chocolate sandwich cookies are everyone's favorite, and who doesn't love dipping them in a glass of icy cold milk? That all-time favorite is the inspiration for Everyone's Favorite Cookie Dump Cake. Top bowls of this cake with a scoop of vanilla ice cream and you will have a rich and decadent version of cookies and milk.

Nonstick cooking spray
15 vanilla cream–filled chocolate sandwich cookies
1 (15.25- to 18-ounce) box white cake mix
1 (12-ounce) can evaporated milk
1 cup semisweet chocolate chips
½ cup (1 stick) unsalted butter, melted
Vanilla ice cream for serving, optional

tip: Substitute dark chocolate chips for the semisweet chocolate chips if you prefer.

Preheat the oven to 350°F. Spray a 9 x 13-inch pan with nonstick cooking spray.

Place the cookies in a zip-top bag. Crush the cookies with a rolling pin to make fine crumbs.

Sprinkle about half of the cookie crumbs evenly over the bottom of the prepared pan. Sprinkle the cake mix evenly over the cookie crumbs. Drizzle the evaporated milk evenly over the cake mix. Sprinkle the rest of the cookie crumbs and the chocolate chips evenly over all. Drizzle the melted butter evenly over the top.

Bake for 40 to 45 minutes or until the cake is set and golden brown. Allow to cool for 15 to 30 minutes.

Spoon into bowls and top, if desired, with vanilla ice cream.

Cookies 'n Cream Dump Cake

MAKES 1 (9 X 13-INCH) CAKE

How does your cookie crumble? Do you crumble them over ice cream, or add them to your favorite creamy milk shake? Maybe they are the crust on your favorite chocolate pie or cheesecake? We think adding crumbled cookies to a chocolate cake, made with cream, is just a natural choice.

Nonstick cooking spray
12 vanilla cream–filled chocolate sandwich cookies
1 (15.25- to 18-ounce) box devil's food cake mix
2 cups sour cream
½ cup heavy cream
¼ cup (½ stick) unsalted butter, sliced into slivers

Preheat the oven to 350°F. Spray a 9 x 13-inch pan with nonstick cooking spray.

Place the cookies in a zip-top bag. Crush the cookies with a rolling pin to make fine crumbs.

Pour the cake mix into the center of the prepared pan. Spoon in the sour cream and heavy cream. Stir until the cake mix is moistened; the batter will be thick. Spread the batter evenly in the pan. Sprinkle the cookie crumbs evenly over the cake batter. Distribute the butter slivers evenly over the top.

Bake for 40 to 45 minutes or until a wooden pick inserted in the center of the cake comes out clean.

tips: If desired, stir the cake mix with the sour cream and heavy cream in a mixing bowl, then spoon the batter into the pan.

TO GLAZE THE CAKE: In a small bowl, blend together 1 cup confectioners' sugar, 1 tablespoon whole milk, and ½ teaspoon pure vanilla extract. Add an additional 2 to 4 teaspoons milk, blending until the glaze is smooth and reaches the desired consistency. Drizzle the glaze over the cooled cake.

Black Forest Dump Cake

MAKES 1 (9 X 13-INCH) CAKE

The story of who baked the first Black Forest Cake is lost in antiquity, but it comes from the Black Forest region in Germany and is named for the dense forests. The classic chocolate cake, often baked in multiple layers, is flavored with Kirschwasser, a cherry brandy, and is topped with whipped cream. This Black Forest Dump Cake captures those luscious flavors, but the good news is that this recipe is so easy you will be out of the kitchen in just moments.

Nonstick cooking spray
1 (16-ounce) package frozen tart, pitted red cherries
¼ cup sugar
1 (21-ounce) can cherry pie filling
1 (15.25- to 18-ounce) box devil's food cake mix
½ teaspoon pure almond extract
1 cup hot brewed coffee
½ cup (1 stick) unsalted butter, sliced into slivers

Preheat the oven to 350°F. Spray a 9 x 13-inch pan with nonstick cooking spray.

Arrange the frozen cherries evenly in the prepared pan. Sprinkle the sugar evenly over the cherries. Spoon the pie filling evenly over the cherries. Sprinkle the cake mix evenly over the fruit.

Stir the almond extract into the coffee. Drizzle the coffee mixture evenly over the cake mix. Distribute the butter slivers evenly over the top.

Bake for 50 to 55 minutes or until set and the edges of the cake begin to pull away from the sides of the pan.

tips: Frost the cake with an 8-ounce carton of thawed frozen whipped topping. Garnish with 7 to 9 drained maraschino cherries. Or if desired, set aside 7 to 9 of the frozen cherries before assembling the cake; let them thaw, drain well, and place them on the whipped topping. For an even more spectacular look, shave a chocolate candy bar with a vegetable peeler and sprinkle the chocolate shavings over the whipped topping.

If desired, drizzle 2 tablespoons kirsch (or Kirshwasser) evenly over the cherries before baking for a classic flavor twist.

Cranberry-Chocolate Dump Cake

MAKES 1 (9 X 13-INCH) CAKE

Roxanne is known far and wide for a luscious chocolate cranberry cake. It is a favorite all winter long—not just during the holidays. This Cranberry-Chocolate Dump Cake captures that wonderful flavor combination.

Nonstick cooking spray
1 (14-ounce) can whole berry cranberry sauce
1½ cups cranberry juice cocktail
1 (15.25- to 18-ounce) box milk chocolate cake mix
½ cup (1 stick) unsalted butter, sliced into slivers
Whipped cream for serving, optional

Preheat the oven to 350°F. Spray a 9 x 13-inch pan with nonstick cooking spray.

Place the cranberry sauce in the prepared pan. Using a spoon, break the cranberry sauce apart and spread it evenly. Pour ¾ cup of the cranberry juice cocktail evenly over the cranberries. Sprinkle the cake mix evenly over the cranberries. Drizzle the remaining ¾ cup cranberry juice cocktail evenly over the cake mix. Distribute the butter slivers evenly over the top.

Bake for 40 to 45 minutes or until set and the edges of the cake begin to pull away from the sides of the pan. Allow to stand 15 minutes before serving.

Go ahead and dollop each serving with whipped cream if you wish. It can't be beat.

Chocolate–Cherry Cola Dump Cake

MAKES 1 (9 X 13-INCH) CAKE

Some folks believe that cherries and cola go together like peanut butter and jelly. If you are part of this camp of believers, this Chocolate–Cherry Cola Dump Cake is for you!

Nonstick cooking spray
2 (15-ounce) cans tart, pitted red cherries, drained
1 (15.25- to 18-ounce) box devil's food cake
1 cup cola-flavored soda
Whipped cream or ice cream for serving, optional

Preheat the oven to 350°F. Spray a 9 x 13-inch pan with nonstick cooking spray.

Place the well-drained cherries in the prepared pan. In a large bowl, stir together the cake mix and the cola. Dollop or "dump" the batter over the cherries.

Bake for 30 to 35 minutes or until a wooden pick inserted in center of the cake comes out clean. Cool for 10 to 15 minutes before serving. This is great served warm but is still tasty at room temperature topped with whipped cream or ice cream.

White Chocolate–Banana Dump Cake

MAKES 1 (9 X 13-INCH) CAKE

Tired of the same old, same old banana bread? Why not shake it up a bit and give this scrumptious new banana and white chocolate combo a try?

Nonstick cooking spray
5 medium bananas (not overripe)
1 (12-ounce) package premium white chips
1 (5-ounce) can evaporated milk
1 (14-ounce) box banana quick bread mix
1 cup pecan pieces
½ cup (1 stick) unsalted butter, melted
Whipped cream or vanilla ice cream for serving, optional

Preheat the oven to 350°F. Spray a 9 x 13-inch pan with nonstick cooking spray.

Slice the bananas crosswise, about ¼ inch thick, and layer them evenly on the bottom of the prepared pan. Sprinkle premium white chips evenly over the bananas. Pour the evaporated milk evenly over all.

Sprinkle the quick bread mix evenly over the chips. Sprinkle the pecans evenly over the quick bread mix. Drizzle the melted butter evenly over the top.

Bake for 40 to 45 minutes until golden brown, making sure the edges of the cake do not get too brown.

Serve warm or at room temperature with a dollop of whipped cream or ice cream, if desired.

✳ *Flavorful Fruits* ✳

Strawberry-Rhubarb Dump Cake

MAKES 1 (9 X 13-INCH) CAKE

Kathy and Roxanne have a fond tradition of picking strawberries together each year. It has become a family affair as husbands and children tag along for the fun and to help carry the sparkling gems back to the cars. Once back in the kitchen, it is a natural choice to prepare the strawberries with rhubarb to celebrate and enjoy the fruits of their labor.

Nonstick cooking spray
1 (16-ounce) package frozen rhubarb slices
1 (16-ounce) package frozen sliced strawberries, no sugar or
   syrup added
⅔ cup sugar
1 (3-ounce) package strawberry gelatin mix
1 cup water
1 (15.25- to 18-ounce) box white cake mix
½ cup (1 stick) unsalted butter, melted
Whipped cream or ice cream for serving, optional

tip: Substitute fresh rhubarb or fresh strawberries for the frozen. Check the baking progress and reduce the baking time by 5 to 10 minutes if using fresh fruit.

Preheat the oven to 350°F. Spray a 9 x 13-inch pan with nonstick cooking spray.

Place the rhubarb and strawberry slices evenly in the prepared pan. Sprinkle the sugar evenly over the fruit. Sprinkle evenly with the gelatin. Pour the water evenly over the gelatin. Sprinkle the cake mix evenly over the mixture. Drizzle the melted butter evenly over the top.

Bake for 65 to 75 minutes or until the cake is set and golden brown. Serve warm or at room temperature with dollops of whipped cream or ice cream if desired.

Strawberry-Lemonade Dump Cake

MAKES 1 (8 X 8-INCH) CAKE

It is always fun to think outside the box, no pun intended. Use a lemon bar mix, backward with the crust on top, and you have created a dessert that rivals many. Strawberry-Lemonade Dump Cake makes a welcome addition to any picnic basket.

Nonstick cooking spray
3 large eggs
⅓ cup water
1 (19.35-ounce) box lemon bar mix
1½ cups sliced fresh strawberries
⅔ cup sweetened condensed milk
⅓ cup (5⅓ tablespoons) unsalted butter, melted

tip: Substitute fresh blueberries for the strawberries.

Preheat the oven to 350°F. Spay an 8 x 8-inch square pan with nonstick cooking spray.

Place the eggs, water, and lemon filling from the lemon bar box mix in the prepared pan. Whisk together until blended. Allow to stand for 10 minutes.

Layer the strawberries over the lemon filling mixture. Sprinkle the crust mixture from the lemon bar box mix over the strawberries. Drizzle the sweetened condensed milk evenly over the crust mixture. Drizzle the melted butter evenly over the top.

Bake for 40 to 45 minutes until the cake is golden brown on top. Allow to stand for 30 minutes before serving.

Luscious Lemon Dump Cake

MAKES 1 (9 X 13-INCH) CAKE

Lemon is such a bright and fresh flavor, especially in the spring and summer. We love to serve Luscious Lemon Dump Cake out on the patio or terrace on a bright sunny day.

Nonstick cooking spray
1 (3.4-ounce) package lemon instant pudding mix
1 (10-ounce) jar lemon curd
1½ cups whole milk
1 (15.25- to 18-ounce) box yellow cake mix

LEMON GLAZE
2 cups confectioners' sugar
Finely grated zest of 1 lemon
¼ cup freshly squeezed lemon juice

Preheat the oven to 350°F. Spray a 9 x 13-inch pan with nonstick cooking spray.

Pour the pudding mix into the prepared pan. Add ½ cup of the lemon curd and the milk. Whisk until the pudding is thick and creamy, about 2 minutes. Stir in the cake mix and blend until moistened. Spread the batter evenly in the pan. Using a teaspoon, dollop the remaining lemon curd in small spoonfuls evenly over the cake batter. Swirl with the tip of a table knife.

Bake for 40 to 45 minutes or until a wooden pick inserted in the center of the cake comes out clean. Allow the cake to cool.

MAKE THE GLAZE: In a small bowl, whisk together the confectioners' sugar, lemon zest, and lemon juice. Drizzle over the cooled cake.

tip: When grating the lemon zest, grate just the outer, colored portion of the fruit. The white, or pith, is very bitter.

Heavenly Hash Dump Cake

MAKES 1 (9 X 13-INCH) CAKE

What is heavenly hash? To some, it is ice cream with marshmallows, almonds, and chocolate in it. To Kathy, it is a fruit recipe that her grandma made that combined cherries, pineapple, oranges, and marshmallows. It is truly a family heirloom recipe, for that favorite dish was served as both a salad and a dessert. This Heavenly Hash Dump Cake is based on that old-fashioned, tasty fruit combination.

Nonstick cooking spray
1 (15-ounce) can dark sweet cherries or Royal Ann cherries in
　heavy syrup
1 (15-ounce) can mandarin oranges in light syrup
1 (20-ounce) can pineapple tidbits in juice
1 cup miniature marshmallows
1 (15.25- to 18-ounce) box yellow cake mix
½ cup (1 stick) unsalted butter, sliced into slivers

Preheat the oven to 350°F. Spray a 9 x 13-inch pan with nonstick cooking spray.

Put the cherries with the syrup in the prepared pan.

Drain the oranges and the pineapple, reserving the juices. Measure out 1 cup of the reserved juice. Use remaining juice as desired, or discard.

Place the oranges and pineapple evenly into the pan. Sprinkle the marshmallows evenly over the fruit. Sprinkle the cake mix evenly over the marshmallows. Drizzle 1 cup of the reserved juice evenly over the cake mix. Distribute the butter slivers evenly over the top.

Bake for 40 to 45 minutes or until the cake is set and golden brown.

tips: The cherries used in this recipe are sweet cherries in syrup. Old recipes for heavenly hash fruit salad, which inspired this recipe, called for Royal Ann cherries. Royal Ann cherries are a red blush cherry so they are lighter in color. Dark sweet cherries give a beautiful red accent, but either variety works well and you can use the variety you prefer.

If you wish, substitute 1 (21-ounce) can cherry pie filling for the canned sweet cherries in syrup.

Tropical Mango Dump Cake

MAKES 1 (9 X 13-INCH) CAKE

Tropical breezes, mangoes, oranges, and coconut unite in this wonderful Tropical Mango Dump Cake. Frozen mango cubes are now readily available at most grocery stores and make this dessert especially quick and easy to make.

Nonstick cooking spray

1 (16-ounce) package frozen mango cubes

⅓ cup honey

1 (15.25- to 18-ounce) box butter yellow cake mix

½ cup sweetened flaked coconut

1 cup orange juice

½ cup (1 stick) unsalted butter, sliced into slivers

Preheat the oven to 350°F. Spray a 9 x 13-inch pan with nonstick cooking spray.

Arrange the mango cubes evenly in the prepared pan. Drizzle with the honey. Sprinkle the cake mix evenly over the fruit. Sprinkle the coconut evenly over the cake mix. Drizzle the orange juice evenly over all. Distribute the butter slivers evenly over the top.

Bake for 45 to 50 minutes or until the cake is set and golden brown.

tips: If desired, substitute 2½ to 3 cups of fresh, peeled mango cubes for the frozen. Look in the produce section for bags of peeled, cubed, ready-to-use mango. Check the baking progress and reduce the baking time by 5 to 10 minutes if using fresh fruit.

Substitute yellow cake mix for the butter yellow cake mix, if desired.

Sprinkle ½ cup sliced almonds evenly over the coconut. Proceed as the recipe directs.

Lemon-Blueberry Dump Cake

MAKES 1 (9 X 13-INCH) CAKE

Blueberries are proof that good things come in small packages. These purplish-blue gems are packed with antioxidants and are a natural coupled with lemon. Serve this power-packed cake at breakfast, dinner, or afternoon tea.

Nonstick cooking spray
1 (16- to 19-ounce) box lemon cake mix
1 (3.4-ounce) package vanilla instant pudding mix
3 large eggs
1½ cups water
1½ cups fresh or frozen blueberries

LEMON GLAZE
2 cups confectioners' sugar
Finely grated zest of 1 lemon
¼ cup freshly squeezed lemon juice

Preheat the oven to 325°F. Spray a 9 x 13-inch pan with nonstick cooking spray.

Pour the cake mix and pudding mix into the prepared pan. Add the eggs and water to the mixes and carefully whisk together until smooth. Stir in the blueberries. Spread the batter evenly.

Bake for 45 to 50 minutes or until a wooden pick inserted in the center of the cake comes out clean. Allow the cake to cool.

MAKE THE GLAZE: In a small bowl, whisk together the confectioners' sugar, lemon zest, and lemon juice. Drizzle over the cooled lemon-blueberry cake.

tip: We prefer to make this recipe with lemon cake mix but you could use white cake mix and add 2 tablespoons lemon juice to the batter.

Maple-Apple Dump Cake

MAKES 1 (9 X 13-INCH) CAKE

Roxanne's husband, Bob Bateman, loves all desserts with apples. When the Maple-Apple Dump Cake was developed and tested in her kitchen, he begged her to test it again and again. Bob's birthday treat has been earmarked this year.

Nonstick cooking spray
2 (21-ounce) cans apple pie filling
1 (15.25- to 18-ounce) box spice cake mix
¾ cup (1½ sticks) unsalted butter, sliced into slivers

MAPLE GLAZE
¼ cup maple syrup
1 tablespoon unsalted butter
2 teaspoons whole milk
½ teaspoon pure vanilla extract
½ cup confectioners' sugar

tips: If you are short on time, prepare the apple cake and serve it warm, without the glaze.

À la mode, for sure! Top each piece with a scoop of ice cream, with or without the glaze.

Preheat the oven to 350°F. Spray a 9 x 13-inch pan with nonstick cooking spray.

Spread both cans of pie filling in the prepared pan. Sprinkle the cake mix evenly over the fruit. Distribute the butter slivers evenly over the top.

Bake for 40 to 45 minutes or until the cake is golden. Allow to cool for 30 to 45 minutes.

MAKE THE GLAZE: In a small saucepan, combine the maple syrup, butter, and milk and bring to a boil, stirring constantly. Reduce the heat but maintain a boil; cook, stirring constantly, for 2 to 3 minutes. Remove from the heat. Whisk in the vanilla and confectioners' sugar and continue to whisk for 3 to 5 minutes until the mixture cools and begins to thicken. Allow the mixture to cool slightly, 5 to 10 minutes. Drizzle the glaze evenly over the cake.

Serve the cake warm or at room temperature.

Peach Melba Dump Cake

MAKES 1 (9 X 13-INCH) CAKE

Peaches and raspberries, combined in one luscious dessert, seem to be a natural for summer enjoyment. Add a front porch swing on a warm, summer day and the setting is perfect. Top your dessert bowl with a scoop of vanilla ice cream and you just might be in dessert heaven.

Nonstick cooking spray
2 cups (8 ounces) frozen raspberries
4 cups (16 ounces) frozen peach slices
½ cup raspberry preserves (seedless preferred)
1 (15.25- to 18-ounce) box vanilla or white cake mix
1¼ cups half-and-half
½ cup sliced almonds
¼ cup (½ stick) unsalted butter, melted

Preheat the oven to 350°F. Spray a 9 x 13-inch pan with nonstick cooking spray.

Arrange the fruit evenly in the prepared pan. Spoon the preserves evenly over the fruit. Sprinkle the cake mix evenly over the fruit. Pour the half-and-half evenly over the cake mix. Sprinkle the almonds evenly over all. Drizzle the melted butter evenly over the top.

Bake for 50 to 55 minutes or until the cake is golden brown and the fruit is tender.

tips: You can substitute equal amounts of sliced, fresh peaches and fresh raspberries for the frozen. Check the baking progress and reduce the baking time by 5 to 10 minutes if using fresh fruit.

If desired, sprinkle the baked cake with confectioners' sugar and garnish with fresh raspberries.

Apricot Walnut Dump Cake

MAKES 1 (9 X 13-INCH) CAKE

The recipe for Apricot Walnut Dump Cake became a beloved family heirloom when Kathy's aunt shared the recipe many years ago. It was served often since everyone loved the cake, and it was especially sweet knowing it was Aunt Theda's recipe. That special aunt will soon be celebrating her 100th birthday. This recipe continues to delight us all.

Nonstick cooking spray
2 (15.25-ounce) cans apricot halves in syrup
1 (15.25- to 18-ounce) box yellow cake mix
¾ cup chopped walnuts
½ cup (1 stick) unsalted butter, sliced into slivers
Vanilla ice cream for serving, optional

tip: Substitute sliced almonds for the walnuts.

Preheat the oven to 350°F. Spray a 9 x 13-inch pan with nonstick cooking spray.

Pour both cans of the apricots with the syrup into the prepared pan and distribute the apricot halves evenly, cut-side down. Sprinkle the cake mix evenly over the apricots. Sprinkle the walnuts evenly over all. Distribute the butter slivers evenly over the top.

Bake for 40 to 45 minutes or until the cake is set and golden brown.

Serve with a scoop of vanilla ice cream on top if you like.

Apple Butter–Walnut Dump Cake

MAKES 1 (9 X 13-INCH) CAKE

Sometimes it seems that fall afternoons might be too busy for baking. Not so! This wonderful dessert has all of those classic fall flavors you crave, yet takes just minutes to prepare.

Nonstick cooking spray
1 (21-ounce) can apple pie filling
1 Granny Smith apple, peeled, cored, and thinly sliced
½ cup apple butter
1 (15.25- to 18-ounce) box spice cake mix
½ cup chopped walnuts
¾ cup (1½ sticks) unsalted butter, melted
Cinnamon or vanilla ice cream for serving, optional

Preheat the oven to 350°F. Spray a 9 x 13-inch pan with nonstick cooking spray.

Spread the apple pie filling evenly in the prepared pan. Arrange the apple slices evenly over the pie filling. Dollop with the apple butter.

Sprinkle the cake mix evenly over the fruit. Sprinkle the walnuts evenly over all. Drizzle the melted butter evenly over the top.

Bake for 40 to 45 minutes or until the cake is set and golden brown.

Allow to cool for 10 minutes.

Spoon into individual dessert dishes. If desired, serve with a scoop of cinnamon or vanilla ice cream.

Pear and Walnut Dump Cake

MAKES 1 (9 X 13-INCH) CAKE

Pears are great to eat fresh, but when did you last bake with them? Until recently, it seemed that they rarely starred in a luscious baked dessert. Times have changed and pears today are featured in pies, tarts, and wonderful sweet treats, like this one.

Nonstick cooking spray
¾ cup (1½ sticks) unsalted butter, melted
2 (15.25-ounce) cans sliced pears in heavy syrup, drained
¼ cup packed brown sugar
1 (15.25- to 18-ounce) box spice cake mix
1 (12-ounce) can ginger ale
¾ cup chopped walnuts

Preheat the oven to 350°F. Spray a 9 x 13-inch pan with nonstick cooking spray.

Drizzle ¼ cup of the melted butter in the prepared pan and tilt the pan to coat the bottom evenly. Arrange the pears evenly in a single layer in the pan. Sprinkle the brown sugar evenly over the pears. Sprinkle the cake mix evenly over the pears. Pour the ginger ale evenly over the cake mix. Sprinkle the walnuts evenly over all. Drizzle the remaining ½ cup melted butter evenly over the top.

Bake for 40 to 45 minutes until the cake is set and golden brown.

tips: Substitute 2 fresh pears, peeled, cored, and thinly sliced for the canned pears. Increase the brown sugar to ½ cup.

If desired, substitute lemon-lime soda for ginger ale.

Applesauce Gingerbread Dump Cake

MAKES 1 (8 X 8-INCH) CAKE

Another way to say "autumn" is applesauce gingerbread. A cold, blustery day begs you to spend 10 minutes in the kitchen and prepare dessert for those you love. Top each serving with sweetened whipped cream and memories will be made.

Nonstick cooking spray
1 (24-ounce) jar chunky applesauce
1 (14.5-ounce) box gingerbread cake and cookie mix
½ cup (1 stick) unsalted butter, sliced into slivers

Preheat the oven to 350°F. Spray an 8 x 8-inch pan with nonstick cooking spray.

Pour the applesauce evenly into the prepared pan. Sprinkle the gingerbread mix evenly over the applesauce. Distribute the butter slivers evenly over the top.

Bake for 30 to 35 minutes or until the cake is set and golden brown.

tip: There are many varieties of applesauce available in the super-market today. Substitute 24 ounces of your favorite for the chunky applesauce in the recipe.

Pineapple Upside-Down Dump Cake

MAKES 2 (9-INCH) ROUND CAKES

It is time to update classic Pineapple Upside-Down Cake. This lightning-fast version of that timeless cake can't be beat. It is beautiful and tastes just as good as it looks. No one will ever guess you made it in just moments.

Nonstick cooking spray
10 tablespoons (1 stick plus 2 tablespoons) unsalted
    butter, melted
⅔ cup packed brown sugar
2 (15-ounce) cans sliced pineapple in juice, drained,
    reserving juice
10 to 14 maraschino cherries, drained (optional)
1 (3.4-ounce) package vanilla instant pudding mix
¾ cup whole milk
1 (15.25- to 18-ounce) box yellow cake mix

Preheat the oven to 350°F. Line two 9-inch round cake pans with parchment paper. Spray the pans with nonstick cooking spray.

Drizzle 3 tablespoons of the melted butter into each prepared pan and tilt the pans to coat the bottom evenly. Sprinkle ⅓ cup of the brown sugar evenly in each pan.

Arrange the pineapple slices from one can in a single layer in one pan. Arrange 5 to 7 cherries evenly around the pineapple, if desired. Repeat with the second pan.

Measure out 1 cup of the reserved pineapple juice. Use the remaining juice as desired, or discard. In a large bowl, combine the pudding mix with the 1 cup juice and the milk. Whisk until the pudding is thick and creamy, about 2 minutes. Stir in the cake mix and blend until moistened. Spoon half of the batter over

(continued)

Pineapple Upside-Down Dump Cake (continued)

the pineapple in each of the pans and spread evenly. Drizzle 2 table-spoons of the remaining melted butter evenly over the top of the cake batter in each of the pans.

Bake for 35 to 40 minutes or until a wooden pick inserted in the center of each cake comes out clean.

Let cool for 15 minutes. Run a table knife around the outside edges of each cake, then invert onto serving plates. Remove the parchment paper. Serve warm.

Easy-Peasy Cinnamon-Peach Dump Cake

MAKES 1 (11¾ X 7¼-INCH) CAKE

Cinnamon rolls never had it so good! Easy-Peasy Cinnamon-Peach Dump Cake comes together in seconds and the result will rival the corner bakery.

1 (12.4-ounce) tube refrigerated cinnamon rolls with icing
1 (16-ounce) package frozen sliced peaches
1 (9-ounce) box golden yellow cake mix
½ cup (1 stick) unsalted butter, melted

Preheat the oven to 325°F. Spray an 11¾ x 7¼-inch oblong baking dish with nonstick cooking spray.

Arrange the cinnamon rolls evenly in the prepared dish with the dark cinnamon side facing up. Using your fingers, form a cinnamon roll crust on the bottom of the pan by flattening the cinnamon rolls together. Sprinkle evenly with the frozen peaches. Sprinkle the cake mix evenly over the peaches. Drizzle the melted butter evenly over the top.

Line a baking sheet with 1-inch sides with aluminum foil. Place the peach cake, in its baking dish, on the prepared baking sheet.

Bake for 60 to 70 minutes or until the cake is set and golden brown around the edges. Allow to stand for 5 to 10 minutes.

Put the frosting from the cinnamon rolls into a small plastic zip-top bag; clip the corner. Drizzle the frosting over the top of the cake.

tips: It is important to use the right size baking pan or the mixture may boil over. To be safe, always bake on a lined, rimmed baking sheet.

You can substitute 2 cups peeled, pitted, and sliced fresh peaches for the frozen. Check the baking progress and reduce the baking time by 5 to 10 minutes if using fresh fruit.

This recipe calls for a one-layer-size cake mix. If desired, you can use half of a regular, two-layer-size cake mix and reserve the other half of the cake mix for another time.

✳ Caramel and Ooey-Gooey Treats ✳

Peanut Butter Cup Dump Cake

MAKES 1 (9 X 13-INCH) CAKE

Luscious chocolate and peanut butter make a beloved food combo! Your family may crowd near this rich and wonderful Peanut Butter Cup Dump Cake in hopes of nabbing the first piece.

Nonstick cooking spray
3 (3.5-ounce) cartons prepared chocolate pudding
⅓ cup creamy peanut butter
1 (8-ounce) package unwrapped mini peanut butter cup candies
1 (15.25- to 18-ounce) box chocolate fudge cake mix
1 (13-ounce) can evaporated milk
½ cup (1 stick) unsalted butter, sliced into slivers

Preheat the oven to 350°F. Spray a 9 x 13-inch pan with nonstick cooking spray.

Spoon the pudding into the prepared pan and spread to make a thin, even layer. Using a teaspoon, dollop the peanut butter evenly over the pudding. Sprinkle the peanut butter cup candies evenly over the peanut butter. Sprinkle the cake mix evenly over the candy. Drizzle the evaporated milk evenly over the cake mix. Distribute the butter slivers evenly over the top.

Bake for 40 to 45 minutes or until set.

tips: If desired, substitute 1½ cups of chopped unwrapped peanut butter cup candies for the package of mini candies.

If desired, substitute 1¼ cups half-and-half for the evaporated milk.

Substitute crunchy peanut butter for the creamy peanut butter.

Garnish, if desired, with chopped peanuts, chocolate chips, or additional peanut butter cup candies. Sprinkle the garnishes over the top of the cake just before baking.

Salted Caramel Chocolate Dump Cake

MAKES 1 (9 X 13-INCH) CAKE

Aren't you glad sprinkling caramel and chocolate with sea salt has become popular? The sweet, salty, and tangy flavor sensation creates happiness each and every time.

Nonstick cooking spray
1 (15.25- to 18-ounce) box devil's food cake mix
1 (3.9-ounce) package chocolate instant pudding mix
1¾ cups whole milk
1 (14-ounce) package caramels, unwrapped
Coarse sea salt for sprinkling
Whipped cream for serving, optional

Preheat the oven to 350°F. Spray a 9 x 13-inch pan with nonstick cooking spray.

In a large bowl, whisk together the cake and pudding mixes. Add the milk and whisk until smooth. Spread the batter evenly in the prepared pan.

Using kitchen scissors, carefully cut each caramel in half. Sprinkle the caramel halves evenly over the cake batter. Sprinkle evenly with the sea salt. (Use the sea salt sparingly as you do not want too much.)

Bake for 30 to 35 minutes or until the edges of the cake begin to pull away from the sides of the pan or a wooden pick inserted in the center in between caramels comes out clean.

Place on a cooling rack and allow to cool slightly. This recipe is best served warm. If allowed to cool completely, the caramels will become solid and chewy.

Serve with a dollop of whipped cream if desired.

Candy Bar Dump Cake

MAKES 1 (9 X 13-INCH) CAKE

You might ask if the Candy Bar Dump Cake is a cake or candy bar. There is no need to ponder that question very long, for this rich dessert will remind you of both! Be prepared, as family members may swarm around this incredible dessert, dig in, and just may forget to share.

Nonstick cooking spray
½ cup (1 stick) unsalted butter, melted
6 (1.86-ounce) milk chocolate–covered nougat, caramel, and
    peanut candy bars, such as Snickers, sliced crosswise into
    ¼-inch pieces
1 cup roasted salted peanuts
1 cup semisweet chocolate chips
¾ cup thick butterscotch caramel topping (see tips)
1 (15.25- to 18-ounce) box devil's food cake mix
1¼ cups half-and-half

Preheat the oven to 350°F. Spray a 9 x 13-inch pan with nonstick cooking spray.

Drizzle 2 tablespoons of the butter into the prepared pan and tilt the pan to coat the bottom evenly. Arrange the candy bar pieces evenly in the pan. Sprinkle about half of the peanuts and chocolate chips evenly over the candy bar pieces. Drizzle the caramel topping evenly over the peanuts and the chocolate chips.

Sprinkle the cake mix evenly over the caramel. Drizzle the half-and-half evenly over the cake mix. Drizzle the remaining 6 tablespoons melted butter over the top.

Bake for 40 to 45 minutes or until set and golden brown.

tips: Serve this candy cake warm by spooning it into individual dessert dishes. It is also good if cooled, but you will find it easier to serve the cooled cake if you line the pan with parchment paper, then spray it with nonstick cooking spray. Plan ahead, so if you are taking this cake to a potluck party, family reunion, or picnic, line the pan with parchment paper before baking to make serving easier.

Ice cream topping or syrup? While similar, those labeled "ice cream topping" are thicker than syrups. For the best results for this recipe, choose a thick ice cream topping. We prefer Mrs. Richardson's brand Butterscotch Caramel topping, as it gave the best results.

Southern Praline Dump Cake

MAKES 1 (9 X 13-INCH) CAKE

A trip to New Orleans always has to include samples of freshly made pralines, the famous local candy that features butter, brown sugar, and pecans. Southern Praline Dump Cake is inspired by those rich candies. It reminds us of our fun trips to that renowned city and all of the great food we've enjoyed there. Serve up a big, warm piece and savor the flavor!

Nonstick cooking spray
1 (3.4-ounce) package vanilla instant pudding mix
1¾ cups whole milk
1 (15.25- to 18-ounce) box butter pecan cake mix
1 cup chopped pecans, toasted
⅓ cup packed brown sugar
¼ cup (½ stick) unsalted butter, melted

PRALINE GLAZE
1 tablespoon unsalted butter
¼ cup packed brown sugar
2 tablespoons heavy cream
½ teaspoon pure vanilla extract

Preheat the oven to 350°F. Spray a 9 x 13-inch pan with nonstick cooking spray.

In a large bowl, combine the pudding mix and milk. Whisk until the pudding is thick and creamy, about 2 minutes. Stir in the cake mix and blend until moistened. Spoon half of the batter into the prepared pan and spread to cover the pan evenly.

In a small bowl, stir together the pecans, brown sugar, and 2 tablespoons of the melted butter. Using a teaspoon, dollop half of the pecan mixture, in small spoonfuls, evenly over the cake batter.

Spoon the remaining cake batter, in dollops, evenly over the pecans. Dollop with the remaining pecan mixture. Drizzle the remaining 2 tablespoons melted butter evenly over the top.

✳ **tip:** If you omit the Praline Glaze, this cake becomes an irresistible butter-pecan coffee cake and is ideal for brunch.

Bake for 35 to 40 minutes or until a wooden pick inserted in the center of the cake comes out clean. Allow to cool for 15 minutes.

MAKE THE GLAZE: Place the butter in a microwave-safe 1-cup glass bowl or cup. Microwave on High (100%) power for 30 to 40 seconds or until the butter has melted. Stir in the brown sugar and microwave on High for 30 seconds. Stir well and continue to microwave for 10 seconds or until the sugar has melted and the mixture is bubbling and hot. Stir in the cream. Microwave on High for 10 seconds or until the mixture bubbles and is hot. Stir until the sauce is smooth. Stir in the vanilla. Drizzle the glaze over the cake.

Cinnamon Roll Dump Cake

MAKES 1 (9 X 9-INCH) CAKE

Cinnamon Roll Dump Cake is the ideal sweet treat for a brunch or holiday breakfast and is best served while warm. It is so easy you can put it in the oven even on the busiest morning while you are getting ready for your day, then you can share a warm treat with your family and friends.

Nonstick cooking spray
1 (12.4-ounce) tube refrigerated cinnamon rolls with icing
1 (13.9-ounce) box cinnamon streusel muffin mix
1 cup cinnamon-flavored liquid coffee creamer
½ cup (1 stick) unsalted butter, melted

Preheat the oven to 350°F. Spray a 9 x 9-inch square pan with nonstick cooking spray.

Arrange the cinnamon rolls evenly in the prepared pan with the dark cinnamon side facing up.

Sprinkle the muffin mix evenly over the rolls. (Reserve the streusel package from the muffin mix.) Drizzle the coffee creamer evenly over the muffin mix. Drizzle the melted butter evenly over the top. Sprinkle the reserved streusel mix evenly over the top.

Bake for 40 to 45 minutes or until the cake is set and golden brown. Allow to cool for 5 to 10 minutes.

Put the frosting from the cinnamon rolls into a small plastic zip-top bag; clip the corner. Drizzle the frosting over the cake. Serve warm.

tip: Use your favorite flavor of liquid coffee creamer in this recipe or substitute half-and-half for the coffee creamer.

Peanut Butter Cream Dump Cake

MAKES 1 (9 X 13-INCH) CAKE

It is time to admit your true peanut butter addiction. Do you reach for the jar of peanut butter and eat spoonful after spoonful, straight from the jar? Or do you reach for cookies or pretzels to dip into the jar so that each taste of peanut butter has a sweet crunch? Either way, this Peanut Butter Cream Dump Cake is for you and will ease your peanut butter cravings.

Nonstick cooking spray
¾ cup (1½ sticks) unsalted butter, melted
1 (10-ounce) package peanut butter chips
⅔ cup creamy peanut butter
1 (15.25- to 18-ounce) box yellow cake mix
1 (12-ounce) can evaporated milk

Preheat the oven to 350°F. Spray a 9 x 13-inch pan with nonstick cooking spray.

Drizzle ¼ cup of the melted butter into the prepared pan and tilt the pan to coat the bottom evenly. Sprinkle about half of the peanut butter chips evenly over the butter. Using a teaspoon, dollop the peanut butter evenly over the chips. Sprinkle the cake mix evenly over the peanut butter. Drizzle the milk evenly over the cake mix. Sprinkle the remaining half of the peanut butter chips evenly over all. Drizzle the remaining ½ cup melted butter evenly over the top.

Bake for 40 to 45 minutes or until the cake is set and golden brown.

tips: Substitute crunchy peanut butter, if desired.

Just before baking, sprinkle with ¾ cup of salted roasted peanuts, if desired.

Toffee Crunch Dump Cake

MAKES 1 (9 X 13-INCH) CAKE

If you are looking for buckets full of kudos at your next dinner party or family gathering, Toffee Crunch Dump Cake is your go-to recipe. Rave reviews each and every time, guaranteed.

Nonstick cooking spray
1 (15.25- to 18-ounce) box German chocolate cake mix
1 (14-ounce) can sweetened condensed milk
1 cup hot brewed coffee
1 (12.25-ounce) jar caramel topping
1 (8-ounce) container frozen whipped topping, thawed
5 to 6 (1.4-ounce) milk chocolate English toffee bars, crushed

tip: Change this version by substituting butterscotch sauce for the caramel sauce. Sprinkle with 5 or 6 crispy crunchy peanut butter candy bars that have been crushed.

Preheat the oven to 350°F. Spray a 9 x 13-inch pan with nonstick cooking spray.

In a large bowl, combine the cake mix, sweetened condensed milk, and coffee until blended. Spoon into the prepared pan and spread evenly.

Bake for 25 to 30 minutes or until a wooden pick inserted in the center of the cake comes out clean or the edges of the cake begin to pull away from the sides of the pan. Place the cake on a cooling rack and let cool completely.

Drizzle the caramel topping evenly over the cooled cake. Spread the whipped topping over the caramel layer and sprinkle evenly with the crushed milk chocolate English toffee bars. Refrigerate for several hours or overnight before serving.

Dulce de Leche Dump Cake

MAKES 1 (9 X 13-INCH) CAKE

Dulce de leche, that thick, rich, caramel-like sauce from South America, Central America, and Mexico, is gaining in popularity all across the USA and we are glad it is because it is so good. This Dulce de Leche Dump Cake is so rich and moist that you won't have to seek out a Latin American bakery again.

Nonstick cooking spray
1 (3.4-ounce) package instant vanilla pudding mix
1 (13.4-ounce) can dulce de leche
1½ cups whole milk
1 (16- to 19-ounce) box caramel cake mix
¼ cup (½ stick) unsalted butter, sliced into slivers
¼ cup heavy cream

Preheat the oven to 350°F. Spray a 9 x 13-inch pan with nonstick cooking spray.

Pour the pudding mix into the prepared pan. Add ½ cup of the dulce de leche and the milk. Whisk until the pudding is thick and creamy, about 2 minutes. Stir in the cake mix, blending until moistened. Spread the batter evenly in the pan.

Dollop ¼ cup of the dulce de leche, by small spoonfuls, evenly over the cake batter and swirl using the tip of a table knife. Distribute the butter slivers evenly over the top.

Bake for 40 to 45 minutes or until a wooden pick inserted in the center of the cake comes out clean. Allow to cool for 15 minutes.

Place the cream and the remaining ¼ cup dulce de leche in a microwave-safe 2-cup glass bowl or cup. Microwave on High (100%) power for 1 minute or until hot and bubbly. Stir to blend well. Drizzle the glaze over the cake.

tips: Dulce de leche, which translates to "sweet milk" is made from milk that cooks so long it becomes thick, sweet, and golden in color. It is now readily available canned or jarred so is easy to use in your recipes. Look for it in larger grocery stores, shelved with Latin American foods or with the evaporated milk.

Instead of drizzling the dulce de leche glaze over the baked cake, top each piece of cake with a scoop of ice cream, then drizzle with the warm dulce de leche glaze.

Sticky Toffee Date Dump Cake

MAKES 1 (9 X 13-INCH) CAKE

Suddenly Sticky Toffee Pudding is trendy and popular in many restaurants. The original dessert was an English pudding, but to those of us in the United States, it is better described as a moist cake filled with dates and topped with toffee sauce. Now those flavors are captured in this easy-to-make dessert.

Nonstick cooking spray
1 cup chopped dried dates
½ cup boiling water
1 (15.25- to 18-ounce) box spice cake mix
1¼ cups half-and-half
1 (8-ounce) package milk chocolate toffee bits
½ cup (1 stick) unsalted butter, sliced into slivers
Caramel syrup for serving, optional

Preheat the oven to 350°F. Spray a 9 x 13-inch pan with nonstick cooking spray.

Distribute the dates evenly in the prepared pan. Pour the boiling water evenly over the dates. Set aside and allow to stand for 5 minutes.

Sprinkle the cake mix evenly over the dates. Drizzle the half-and-half evenly over the cake mix. Sprinkle the toffee bits evenly over all. Distribute the butter slivers evenly over the top.

Bake for 40 to 45 minutes or until the cake is set and golden brown.

If desired, spoon into serving bowls and drizzle with caramel syrup.

tips: Are you familiar with dates? Packages of chopped dried dates are readily available and are typically found on the grocery store shelves near the raisins and other dried fruits. You can also purchase whole, pitted dates; chop them into ¼-inch pieces and measure 1 cup chopped dates.

Substitute 4 to 5 crushed milk chocolate English toffee bars for the toffee bits.

✳ *Specialty Dump Cakes* ✳

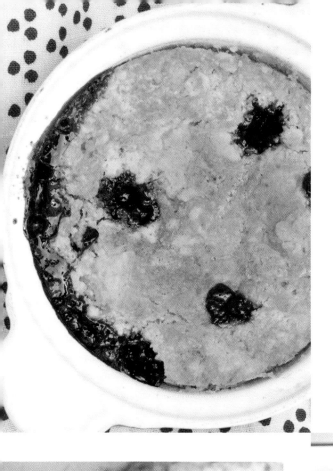

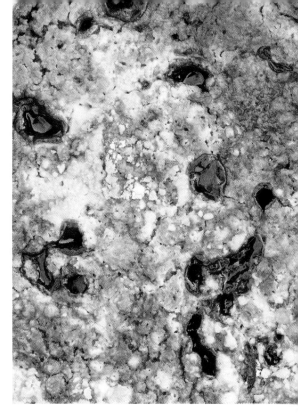

Slow Cooker Apple Spice Dump Cake

MAKES 8 TO 10 SERVINGS

Crisp fall days, apples, and the luscious smell of baking spice cake go together in perfect harmony. Keep it simple, but make the day special with this great-tasting, easy apple cake.

Nonstick cooking spray
2 (14-ounce) packages mixed fresh apple slices (do not peel)
1 cup applesauce
¼ cup packed brown sugar
1 (15.25- to 18-ounce) box spice cake mix
½ cup (1 stick) unsalted butter, sliced into slivers
Ice cream for serving, optional

Spray a 4-quart slow cooker with nonstick cooking spray.

Place the apple slices in the slow cooker. Spoon the applesauce over the apples, then sprinkle with the brown sugar.

Sprinkle the cake mix evenly over the fruit. Distribute the butter slivers evenly over the top.

Cover the slow cooker and bake on High for 2 to 2½ hours or until the fruit is tender, the cake is set, and a wooden pick inserted into the center comes out clean. Serve warm. Top each serving with a scoop of ice cream, if desired.

tips: Sprinkle the applesauce with 1 teaspoon ground cinnamon if a spicier dish is preferred.

Sprinkle 1 cup fruit and nut granola, or ¾ cup chopped toasted pecans or walnuts over the cake mix before baking. Proceed as the recipe directs.

Substitute 8 (4-ounce) containers chopped apples, drained, for the apple slices.

Substitute 5 medium apples, cored and sliced (or about 7 cups of sliced apples) for the packaged apple slices. Toss the apple slices in 1 teaspoon of fresh lemon juice, then proceed as the recipe directs. Increase the sugar to ⅓ to ½ cup packed brown sugar if tart apples are used.

The packaged, sliced apples have a variety of apples included and are not peeled. If slicing your own apples, you may want to peel the apples; the choice is yours.

Anytime Slow Cooker Summer Peach Dump Cake

MAKES 8 TO 10 SERVINGS

You don't need to plan a trip to Georgia, the state known for the best ever peaches, or wait until the dog days of summertime to enjoy the taste of peaches year-round. Your slow cooker can generate summer memories when the temperature drops and the snowflakes are swirling.

Nonstick cooking spray
2 (16-ounce) packages frozen peach slices
1 tablespoon quick-cooking tapioca
1 (15.25- to 18-ounce) box spice cake mix
½ cup (1 stick) unsalted butter, sliced into slivers
½ cup packed brown sugar
½ cup old-fashioned oats
¼ teaspoon ground cinnamon
1 cup chopped pecans, toasted

tip: By all means use fresh peaches if they are available. Substitute 6 to 7 cups peeled, pitted, and sliced fresh peaches for frozen.

Spray a 4-quart slow cooker with nonstick cooking spray.

Place the peaches in the slow cooker and toss with the tapioca. Sprinkle the cake mix evenly over the peaches. Distribute the butter slivers evenly over the top.

In a small bowl, combine the brown sugar, oats, cinnamon, and pecans. Sprinkle the mixture evenly over the butter slivers.

Cover the slow cooker and bake on High for 2 to 3 hours or until the peaches are tender and the topping is set.

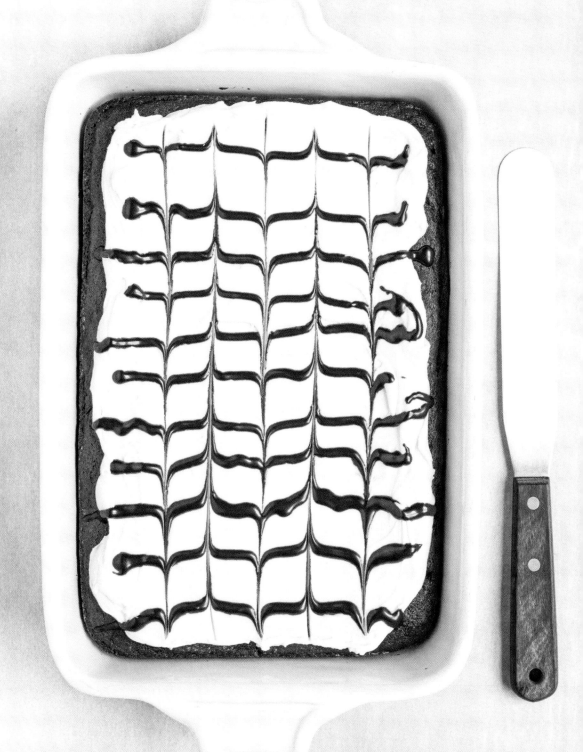

Crème de Menthe Dump Cake

One of Roxanne's fondest memories as a teenager was indulging in ice cream with crème de menthe liqueur drizzled on top. Her parents would carefully pour about 1 tablespoon over chocolate or vanilla ice cream and it seemed like the world stopped for just a moment. Today, she wouldn't serve liqueur to a child but she would definitely serve this Crème de Menthe Dump Cake with light green frosting and a chocolate drizzle to encourage squeals of delight from the children in her home.

Nonstick cooking spray
1 (15.25- to 18-ounce) box dark chocolate or chocolate cake mix
1 (5.9-ounce) package chocolate instant pudding mix
1¾ cups whole milk
1 (10-ounce) package crème de menthe baking chips

CRÈME DE MENTHE FROSTING
½ cup (1 stick) unsalted butter, at room temperature
3½ to 4 cups confectioners' sugar
3 to 4 tablespoons whole milk
1 teaspoon peppermint extract
Few drops of green food coloring
Chocolate syrup for drizzling

tips: We prefer Andes Crème de Menthe baking chips for this recipe. If you desire, substitute mint chips for crème de menthe chips.

Can't find any type of mint chip? Substitute semisweet chocolate chips and add 1 teaspoon peppermint extract to the batter.

Preheat the oven to 350°F. Spray a 9 x 13-inch pan with nonstick cooking spray.

In a large bowl, stir together the cake mix, pudding mix, and milk until smooth. Stir in the crème de menthe chips. Spoon the batter into the prepared pan and spread evenly.

Bake for 25 to 30 minutes or until the edges of the cake begin to pull away from the sides of the pan. Allow the cake to cool completely before serving.

(continued)

MAKE THE FROSTING: In a large bowl, using a mixer on medium-high speed, beat together the butter, 3½ cups of the confectioners' sugar, 3 tablespoons of the milk, the peppermint extract, and a few drops of green food coloring to tint the frosting a mint green color, until light and fluffy. If needed, beat in the remaining ½ cup confectioners' sugar and/or the remaining 1 tablespoon milk to make the frosting the desired consistency. Spread the frosting over the cooled cake.

Drizzle the chocolate syrup in rows on the frosting. Lightly drag a table knife through the chocolate rows to make "v" shapes.

Slow Cooker Pineapple Butter Dump Cake

MAKES 8 TO 10 SERVINGS

Slow cookers, with their low, moist heat, make the best desserts. The pineapple in this dessert caramelizes and makes an unbeatable flavor.

Nonstick cooking spray
2 (20-ounce) cans pineapple tidbits in juice, drained
1 teaspoon ground ginger
¼ cup packed brown sugar
1 (15.25- to 18-ounce) box butter yellow cake mix
½ cup (1 stick) unsalted butter, melted

Spray a 4-quart slow cooker with nonstick cooking spray.

Pour the pineapple from both cans into the slow cooker. Sprinkle with the ginger and the brown sugar.

In a large bowl, mix together the cake mix and the butter with a fork, stirring until the cake mix is moistened and crumbly. Sprinkle the cake mix mixture over the pineapple.

Cover the slow cooker and bake on High for 2 to 2½ hours.

tips: Substitute 1 pineapple, peeled, cored, and cut into ¾- to 1-inch cubes (about 5 cups) or 2 (16-ounce) packages frozen pineapple cubes for the canned pineapple.

Substitute yellow cake mix for the butter yellow cake mix, if desired.

Port 'n Plum Dump Cake

MAKES 1 (9 X 13-INCH) CAKE

This surprising combination may just become your favorite dessert. If you happen to live by one of us, it is a known fact that we will share recipe tests with you. When we shared pieces of this dessert with some friends, they loved it and were surprised to discover that plums were nestled in the cake and that port wine was the secret ingredient. You can also follow the tip to use dried fruit so you can enjoy it year-round.

Nonstick cooking spray

11 tablespoons (1 stick plus 3 tablespoons) unsalted butter, melted

4 to 5 purple plums, pitted and cut into slices about ¼ to ½ inch thick (do not peel)

½ cup sugar

1¼ cups port wine

1 (15.25- to 18-ounce) box white cake mix

Preheat the oven to 350°F. Spray a 9 x 13-inch pan with nonstick cooking spray.

Drizzle 3 tablespoons of the melted butter into the prepared pan and tilt the pan to coat the bottom evenly. Arrange the plum slices evenly in the pan. Sprinkle the sugar evenly over the plums. Drizzle ¼ cup of the port evenly over the sugar. Sprinkle the cake mix evenly over the plums. Drizzle the remaining 1 cup port evenly over the cake mix. Drizzle the remaining ½ cup melted butter over the top.

Bake for 40 to 45 minutes or until the cake is set and golden brown.

tips: The plums do not need peeling. Just pit and slice the fruit.

When plums are not in season, substitute dried plums (known as prunes). Chop 12 to 15 pitted prunes and scatter evenly in the pan. Proceed as the recipe directs.

Port is a sweet red wine and provides a great flavor for this dump cake. If you do not have port, substitute another sweet red wine, sweet vermouth, or Madeira. If you prefer, substitute ¼ cup of grape juice and 1 cup of half-and-half for the 1¼ cups of port. Pour the ¼ cup of juice evenly over the plums and pour 1 cup of half-and-half evenly over the cake mix.

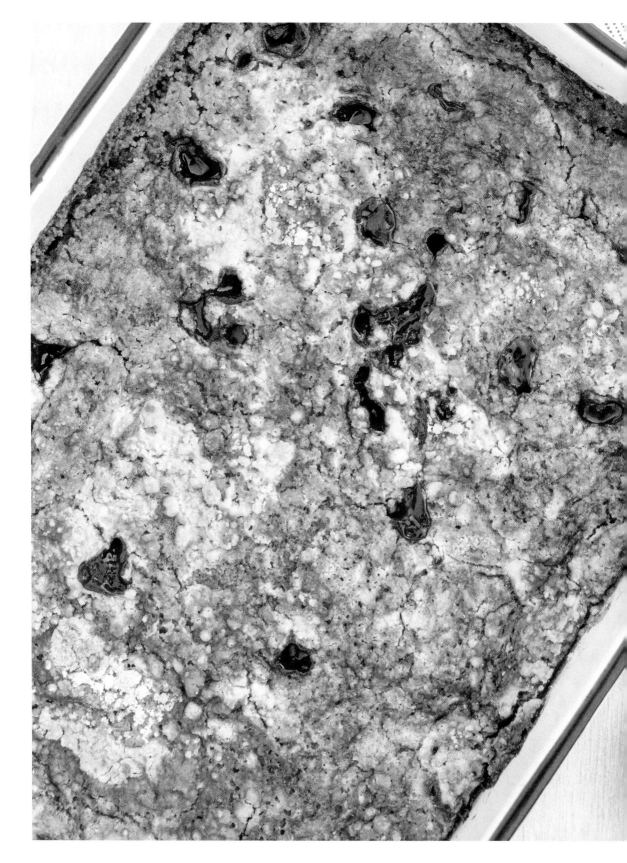

Honey-Fig Bourbon Dump Cake

MAKES 1 (9 X 13-INCH) CAKE

Are you a fan of figs? Suddenly they are a culinary trend, and it is fun to capture their great flavor in all kinds of dishes. From appetizers to desserts, you just might discover that figs are the secret ingredient that gives a recipe a fantastic flavor. Taste this dessert and we bet you will fall in love with the flavor of figs.

Nonstick cooking spray
1 (8-ounce) package dried Mission figs, stems removed,
chopped into ¼-inch pieces
⅔ cup fig preserves
¾ cup boiling water
1 (15.25- to 18-ounce) box yellow cake mix
⅓ cup packed brown sugar
½ cup bourbon
⅓ cup sliced almonds
½ cup (1 stick) unsalted butter, sliced into slivers

Preheat the oven to 350°F. Spray a 9 x 13-inch pan with nonstick cooking spray.

Sprinkle the chopped figs evenly in the prepared pan. Spoon the fig preserves over the figs and stir to blend and distribute evenly in the pan. Pour the boiling water evenly over the figs. Let stand for 5 minutes.

Sprinkle the cake mix evenly over the figs. Sprinkle the brown sugar evenly over the cake mix. Pour the bourbon evenly over all. Sprinkle the sliced almonds evenly over all. Distribute the butter slivers evenly over the top.

Bake for 40 to 45 minutes or until the cake is set and golden brown.

Rum-Raisin Dump Cake

MAKES 1 (9 X 13-INCH) CAKE

We laugh that we can be the best of friends and still enjoy different foods. Raisins are a favorite of Kathy's, but not so much for Roxanne. Guess who serves this dessert often?

Nonstick cooking spray
½ cup (1 stick) unsalted butter, melted
1 cup raisins
½ cup packed brown sugar
1 cup applesauce
1 (15.25- to 18-ounce) box spice cake mix
½ cup golden rum
½ cup chopped pecans

tip: Substitute unsweetened apple juice for the rum in this recipe if you prefer.

Preheat the oven to 350°F. Spray a 9 x 13-inch pan with nonstick cooking spray.

Drizzle 2 tablespoons of the butter into the prepared pan and tilt the pan to coat the bottom evenly. Sprinkle the raisins evenly in the pan. Sprinkle the brown sugar evenly over the raisins. Spoon the applesauce evenly over the raisins. Sprinkle the cake mix evenly over the applesauce. Drizzle the rum evenly over the cake mix. Sprinkle the pecans evenly over all. Drizzle the remaining 6 tablespoons melted butter over the top.

Bake for 40 to 45 minutes or until the cake is set and golden brown.

Blueberry Dump Cake for Two

MAKES 2 SERVINGS

Brunch for two on a lazy Saturday morning or dinner for two after a busy day. Either way, a sweet treat is the perfect ending for a great meal.

Nonstick cooking spray
½ cup fresh blueberries
¼ cup blueberry preserves
1 cup yellow cake mix
¼ cup half-and-half
2 tablespoons unsalted butter, sliced into slivers

Preheat the oven to 350°F. Spray two 8-ounce ramekins (about 3½ inches in diameter and 2¼ inches deep) with nonstick cooking spray. Line a baking sheet with 1-inch sides with aluminum foil.

Spoon half of the blueberries into each ramekin. Top each with 2 tablespoons of the preserves. Sprinkle ½ cup of the cake mix evenly over the blueberries in each ramekin. Drizzle 2 tablespoons of the half-and-half evenly over the cake mix in each ramekin. Distribute the butter slices evenly over the top of each ramekin.

Place the ramekins on the prepared baking sheet.

Bake for 25 to 30 minutes or until the blueberry cakes are set and golden.

(continued)

Blueberry Dump Cake for Two (continued)

tips: Instead of baking two individual servings, you can bake one small cake. Substitute a 6-inch round baking pan about 1½ inches deep or a 3-cup oven-safe casserole dish for the ramekins. Proceed as the recipe directs, layering the ingredients evenly in the pan. Bake for 30 to 35 minutes.

No blueberry preserves? Substitute your favorite berry preserves or honey.

This is a perfect time to make your own cake mix. See pages 10 to 13.

Substitute frozen blueberries for the fresh. No need to thaw the berries. Prepare as directed, baking for 30 to 35 minutes.

Blueberry Mug Cake for One: Spray a microwave-safe 12-ounce glass coffee mug with nonstick cooking spray. Place ½ cup of the cake mix into the mug. Distribute 1 tablespoon of butter slivers evenly over the cake mix. Microwave on High (100%) power for 45 seconds. Stir to moisten the cake mix with the melted butter. Top with ¼ cup blueberries and 2 tablespoons blueberry preserves. (Omit the half-and-half.) Microwave on High (100%) power for 45 to 60 seconds or until bubbly. Allow to stand for 2 minutes.

Pumpkin Bourbon Nut Dump Cake

MAKES 1 (9 X 13-INCH) CAKE

This is the perfect dessert to take to the holiday potluck. Pumpkin, nuts, and a splash of bourbon combine to make a rich, comforting dessert.

Nonstick cooking spray
1 (15-ounce) can pure pumpkin puree
1 (5-ounce) can evaporated milk
¼ cup bourbon
1 (15.25- to 18-ounce) box spice cake mix
⅓ cup packed brown sugar
½ cup chopped walnuts
¾ cup (1½ sticks) unsalted butter, melted
Whipped cream for serving, optional

Preheat the oven to 350°F. Spray a 9 x 13-inch pan with nonstick cooking spray.

Spread the pumpkin puree evenly in the prepared pan. Drizzle the evaporated milk and bourbon evenly over the puree.

Sprinkle the cake mix evenly over the puree. Sprinkle the brown sugar evenly over the cake mix. Sprinkle the walnuts evenly over the brown sugar. Drizzle the butter evenly over the top.

Bake for 35 to 40 minutes or until the cake is set and golden brown. Allow to cool for 10 minutes.

Spoon into individual dessert dishes. Garnish, if desired, with a dollop of whipped cream.

✳ *Acknowledgments* ✳

No cookbook can occur without the help of many people. We want to thank each of you who have contributed so much to this cookbook.

Roxanne's family: Bob Bateman for being a supportive and loving spouse and for always and eagerly grabbing the dish towel to help me with dishes. I love you for always and forever. To our daughter, Grace, you are the light of our world. Thank you for enduring days on end of dessert recipes and grabbing a spoon to taste. The highest compliment I ever receive is when you say, "Mom, will you promise to make this one again?" I love you to the moon and back. To my mom, Colleen Wyss, who taught me that love for friends and family can be expressed by stirring, mixing, and cooking in the kitchen. She is still mixing and sharing after all these years.

Kathy's family: David, Laura, and Amanda, you are my world and mean everything to me. Thank you for your love and support. Your patience as I ask another techy question or again beg you to stop at the grocery store is extraordinary. Your smiles and hugs fill my life with joy and I love you more than words can express.

We have absolutely fantastic agents and cannot thank them enough! Lisa Ekus, Sally Ekus, and the entire staff at The Lisa Ekus Group, LLC, are wonderful and we are grateful for their continued excellent guidance and friendship.

BJ Berti and the St. Martin's Press team are great, and we appreciate all of their creativity, support, and hard work. Thank you for all you do for us and for producing wonderful, beautiful cookbooks.

Staci Valentine is a brilliant photographer and we are so grateful that she shared her talent with us. Her skill, along with that of food stylist Jeanne Kelley, created the most scrumptious photos and made our recipes come to life. Thank you.

We met in a test kitchen over thirty years ago and from that beginning created a rewarding career and a steadfast friendship. We appreciate each other, for we thrive on the brainstorming, tasting, and laughter that friendship gives.

We are grateful for so many friends and colleagues who have nourished and supported us along our path. We know that we could not have accomplished anything without your support. Thank you all.

Please continue to share our journey at www.pluggedintocooking.com.

✳ *Index* ✳